Why the CRAWFISH Lives in the MUD

Why the CRAWFISH Lives in the MUD

Written and Illustrated by
Johnette Downing

PELICAN PUBLISHING COMPANY
GRETNA 2009

For Robbie, John, and Joanna

The word "Pelican" and the depiction of a pelican are trademarks of Pelican Publishing Company, Inc., and are registered in the U.S. Patent and Trademark Office.

Library of Congress Cataloging-in-Publication Data

Downing, Johnette.
  Why the crawfish lives in the mud / written and illustrated by Johnette Downing.
      p. cm.
  Summary: When Crawfish takes advantage of Crab's generosity, his trickery costs him the friendship.
  ISBN 978-1-58980-678-8 (hardcover : alk. paper) [1. Crabs—Fiction. 2. Crayfish—Fiction. 3. Deception—Fiction.] I. Title.
  PZ7.D759277Wh 2009
  [E]—dc22
                                                    2009003959

Printed in Korea
Published by Pelican Publishing Company, Inc.
1000 Burmaster Street, Gretna, Louisiana 70053

Long ago in the waters of the bayou, the crab and the crawfish used to be best friends.

That is, until one hot, muggy day when Crawfish was
feeling more lazy than usual. Crawfish was getting hungry,
but he would not budge an inch to find a meal for himself.

Then Crawfish heard a loud commotion and saw Crab carrying a fish he had just caught in his claws.

Suddenly Crawfish had the *envie*, the craving, for fish, which caused another loud racket in his hungry stomach. Crawfish rubbed his belly, thought for a moment, concocted a plan, and said, "Sure is a hot one, eh Crab?"

"That it is," replied Crab, balancing the fish in one claw and wiping the sweat of hard work from his brow with the other.

"That fish sure looks good," said Crawfish.

"Yes, indeed it does," said Crab.

"Well I declare, you are just too strong to carry such a small fish as that," said Crawfish.

"A small fish?" asked Crab.

"Oh yeah, *cher*," replied Crawfish mockingly, "As strong as you are, you probably can't even feel that small, ti-tiny fish you got yourself there. Now, one of those big fish down the bayou would give you a run for your money."

"Big fish? Bigger than this one?" asked Crab.

"Oh yes, much bigger than that small, ti-tiny, itsy bitsy fish you got yourself there—*beaucoup*, much bigger. Now that big fish down the bayou would be some fine eat'n for you. Yes indeed, some fine eat'n," answered Crawfish.

Crab looked up at his catch of the day and suddenly it didn't feel so heavy and it didn't look so big.

Lazy Crawfish laid it on thick again and said, "Of course, that small, ti-tiny, itsy bitsy, puny fish you got yourself there would be fine eat'n for a weak little crawfish like me, but you, so big and strong, you'd need something bigger, much bigger. But, *c'est la vie*, that's life, I guess I'll go get that big fish down the bayou and try to drag it home. I'll probably hurt my back in the trying."

Crab put down his dinner and said, "Oh no! I wouldn't want you to hurt yourself, dear friend Crawfish. Here, you take my little fish, and I'll go down the bayou and get that big fish."

"You would do that for me?" asked Crawfish, hiding his devious grin.

"Sure, I would," said Crab as he handed his dinner to Crawfish and marched down the bayou.

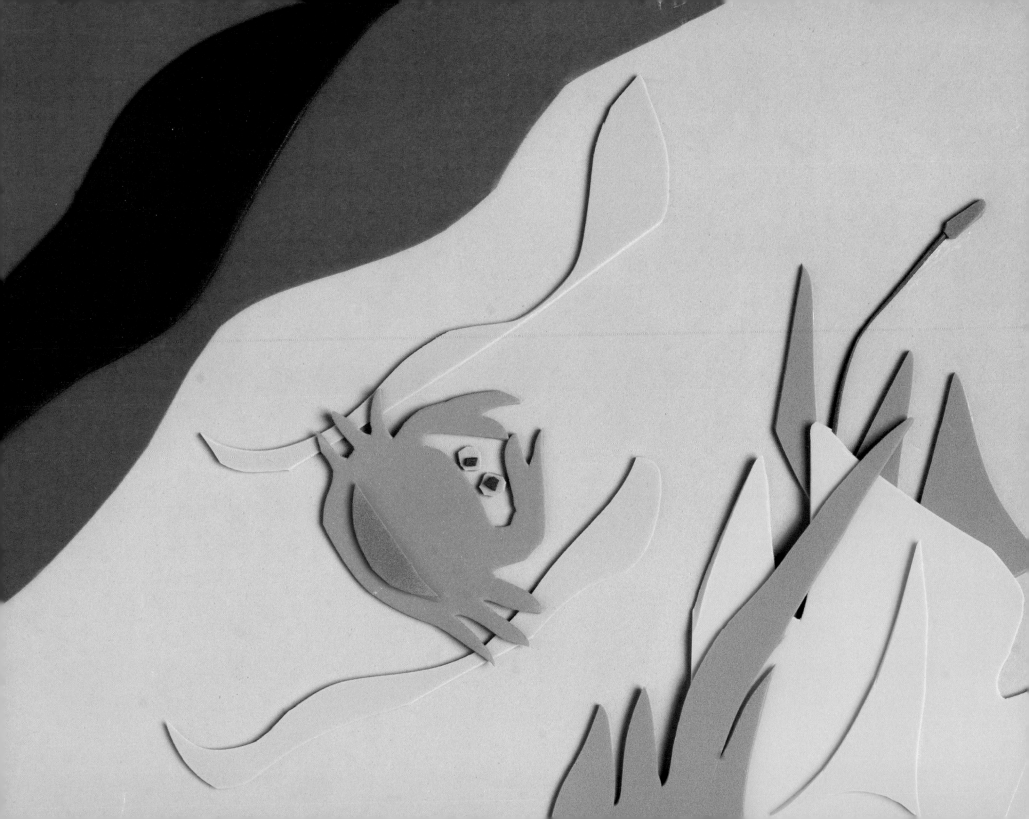

Crawfish laughed and laughed at the foolish Crab. "Ha, ha, ha! I've out-smarted that silly crab again," said Crawfish. He laughed so hard he turned red all over. Then Crawfish ate until he could eat no more, rubbed his full tummy, and took a long nap in the hot, Southern sun.

Click, click, click! Suddenly, Crawfish heard a sound. Click, click, click! The sound came again, but this time it was closer and louder. Crawfish woke from his nap to find angry Crab standing over him clicking his mighty claws together.

Crab yelled, "You lazy, *canaille* trickster! I walked up and down the bayou looking for that big fish and found none."

Crawfish backed up a little 'cause he could tell that Crab was some furious.

Crab said, "You played another dirty trick and made a fool out of me for the last time?"

Crawfish backed up a little bit more. He had never seen Crab this angry before.

Crab continued, "And to think, I gave you my dinner because I felt sorry for you!"

Crawfish backed up a little more and, trying to compose himself, said, "Ah, *mais cher,* I'm just *couillion,* you know, crazy. There's no need for you to be so crabby."

Crab replied, "Crabby? Why, I should throw you into the mud for pulling such a dirty trick on me."

"Oh no, not the mud. I don't like the mud," said Crawfish, "I'll get stuck in the mud and never get out; anything, oh anything, but the mud!"

Now a frightened Crawfish was backing away from Crab so fast and flicking his fantail so frantically that he unknowingly dug a deep tunnel in the mud and fell into it with a PLOP!

Clods of mud encircled the tunnel's entrance, and Crawfish, burrowed inside, was hidden from sight. Crab couldn't believe his eyes.

"Well, I'll be; what goes around, comes around," said Crab, "I guess you've out-smarted yourself this time and got exactly what you deserved. Now the mud will be your home forever."

And to this day, the crawfish, also known as the mudbug, lives in the mud to keep away from the angry crab.

Words and Phrases

Beaucoup (boo koo): much
Canaille (kon-eye): sly or sneaky
C'est la vie (say la vee): that's life
Cher (shaa): dear or friend
Concocted: invented or created
Couillion (koo-yongh): crazy or silly
Envie (ongh-vee): a craving
Mais (meh): but
Laid it on thick: exaggerated
Loud racket: a loud noise
Run for your money: a challenge
Ti-tiny (tee-tiny): very small
What goes around, comes around:
    what you do to others, is done to you

Crawfish Fun Facts

1. Crawfish are freshwater aquatic invertebrates belonging to the crustacean family along with shrimp, crabs, and lobsters.
2. The crawfish is Louisiana's state crustacean.
3. Common names for the crawfish are crayfish, crawdad, and mudbug. The French word for crawfish is *l'écrevisse*.
4. Crawfish are decapods, meaning they have ten legs.
5. The hard outer shell of the crawfish is called the exoskeleton.
6. Crawfish are reddish brown and sometimes blue in color but turn deep red when cooked.
7. Crawfish are omnivores, meaning they eat both plants and animals.
8. Crawfish live in muddy waters, wetlands, marshes, swamps, bayous, and ditches.
9. Crawfish use their claws and fantails to dig tunnels and build mounds.
10. Crawfish mounds are raised earthen cylinder-shaped entrances to the crawfish hole or tunnel and are used as a defense against predators.